THE MONSTERS' RHAPSODY:
Disability, Culture, & Identity

THE MONSTERS' RHAPSODY:
Disability, Culture, & Identity

Ann Magill

Aesop's Pen
2016

First Printing: 2016

ISBN 978-1-365-21201-7

Aesop's Pen
500 Sandcastle Court
Chesapeake, VA 23320

Aesops_Pen@VFEmail.net

DEDICATION

To all the monstrous people:
To those with the courage to roar,
Those who whisper,
Those who sing,
And to those still finding their voice.

In memory of my mother,
Who listened.

To honor the residents of
Tsukui Yamayuri-en:
May I never let the crimes
Against you be forgotten.

Many thanks to ss, whose keen ear for language helped me find the words, and to Jesse the K, whose keen eye helped to put them on the page.

I also (always) thank them both for their friendship, which helped me through the dark.

Contents

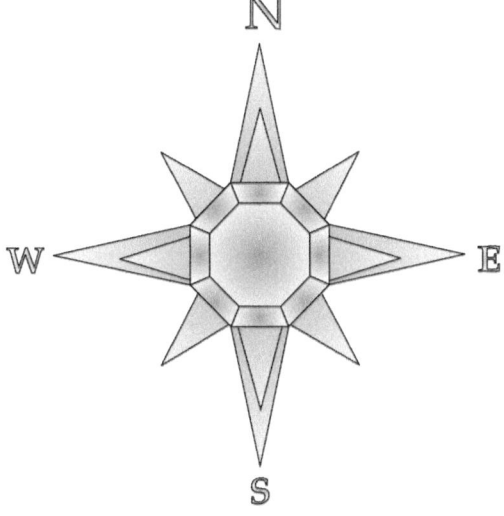

THE MONSTERS' RHAPSODY

We come from regions at the edge of maps
Where details of the landscape are left out.
Those who journey there are warned of traps;
Our histories are vague, and filled with doubt.

We crouch in corners of cathedral towers,
Peering from the ledges high above
Jeering at the milky, gilded saints
With their songs of torment in the key of 'love'.

We gather in the margins of the page,
Drawn there by those minds too quick for text
Cavorting in the space between the lines
And looking out beyond the screen of Time
At what has gone before, and what comes next
With our piercing, wide-eyed, wild, gaze.

Cartographers of power fear us most.
Perhaps by accident, or secret pledge,
They were the ones who pushed us to the edge.
To them, we are the "evil (demon) host."

To curry favor with their patron lords,
They pondered, and they toiled, and they forged
A chain of being strung 'tween God and Earth
To justify the privilege of their birth.
With words of silk, and blood-black ink,
They braided ropes to every link
To bind each living creature into place

Then doled out dwindling portions of God's grace.
But for themselves, they kept the greatest share –
In sight of angels in the shining air.

But we – the vast and secret multitude,
Who move through narrow spaces in between,
Traversing landscapes they have never viewed –
We slip through gaps in their great chain.

We are the *neithers* and the *nors* –
Exceptions to each rule they write:
We are the maids with fishy tails,
Who sing the doom of sailing ships,
And giants, standing miles high,
Who scrape their knees on mountain peaks,
The gryphon, werewolf, and the king
Who's neither frog, nor yet a man.
The mother who can only crawl,
As if she were a tiny babe,
The boy who reads with fingertips,
Poets who shape words with hands,
And those who have divergent minds.
We are the *neithers* and the *nors* –
Exceptions to each rule they write.

And whether shy and shifting, or rudely bold,
We can't be collared by their ready names –
Their inky, silky, fetters do not hold.
They say this is our crime – that we're to blame.

That we exist at all is proof enough
The world is more complex than first it seems
They claimed a single truth. And thus, they lied –
Their mighty chain was forged from human pride,
A false conclusion, and a foolish dream.
But we are here. And we can call their bluff.

And even as we wander city streets,
Along with all the rushing, bustling crowds,
The questions rise in every gaze we meet,
And mystery surrounds us, like a cloud.

We span the borders by which this world's defined –
Not on the globe, but rather, in the mind.

ANTHEM (FOR THE PEOPLE OF NO NATION)

"All borders are invisible from space."
This is our prayer for peace,
Our song of hope,
The story that we tell ourselves,
Trying, with the telling,
To make it so.

Except from space, we see the blazing lights
Tracing out lines of power:
In the capital cities, coiled knots,
Across the deserts, pulled tight and thin.
And all of them bright enough
To hide the stars.

And then there are the borders in the mind
(of which we do not sing):
The boundaries that separate
Those whose mortal weakness
We shall forgive
From those whose weaknesses
Are shamed.

We who dwell behind those lines
Are one in seven.
One in twenty grow up here;
Others immigrate by accident,
Many drift in with advancing age.
We are one billion 'poor, unfortunate, few.'
We have no flag to rally under,

Nor to drape the coffins of our dead.
And even if we had,
What should mark the canton,
And what the fly?

We are as different from each other
As we are from those
Who draw the lines.
Yet when we meet,
Sometimes, we recognize:
We share a common struggle.
We dread a common fate.
And we can even feel
A common pride.

The history I tell is mine.
The landscape I describe,
Its beauty, and its trash,
Is only what I, myself, have seen.
But this is my anthem
For the people of No Nation
(Who dwell in all nations).
This is my prayer for peace,
The story that I tell,
Hoping, with the telling,
To make it so.

FABLES AND PHANTOMS

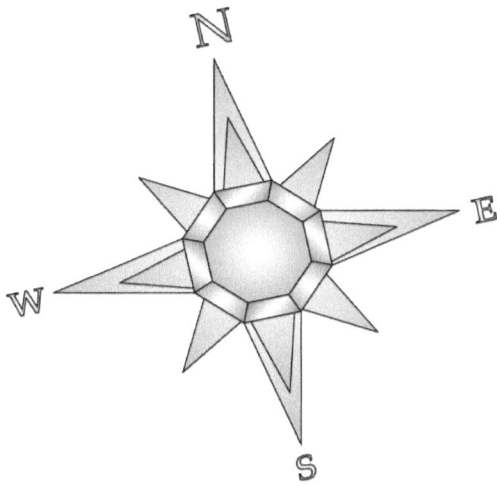

THE FROG KING IN THREE VOICES

FIRST: IRON HEINRICH

We never saw the witch that cast the spell,
Nor heard her incantation in the night.
No shadows lingered at the royal well ...
Yet, what, besides a witch, could cause this fright?
It is a nightmare I will not forget –
To see His Majesty shrink down so small,
His eyes grow large, his skin turn soft and wet;
I swear his cries still echo through the hall.
If not for hope that this may be undone,
I would succumb to grief and welcome death.
Yet I do hope, and pray to God's Own Son,
The king may once again draw human breath.
And so I wear these bands around my heart,
Or else, for pain, 'twould surely break apart.

SECOND: THE LINDEN TREE

I've grown here in this wood for centuries:
Fed honeybees and aphids both alike,
Heard verdicts read, both merciful and cruel,
And suffered lovers' names carved in my bark.
But there is one I never shall forget:
Each summer day, she'd come to me and hide
Her beauty from the jealous, leering, sun
And play a game of catch all by herself.
I was surprised as she to hear the frog

Call out to her with such a human voice.
If only I, like he, could speak so clear,
I would have said: "No plaything's worth the cost."
She ran for home too soon – the sun still high,
And never more returned to grace my shade.

Third: The King

The thrill of fear was almost sweet as lust
When she, in anger, threw me at the wall.
Was it because the penalty was just,
My human form returned upon my fall?
She trembled through the night, but said her tears
Were shed for joy, because I had "kind eyes."
So young to learn the lesson *hide your fears*;
That skill will let the courtiers say: "She's wise."
I told her 'twas a witch that transformed me.
How could I tell her that I knew not why?
They say that truth will always set you free,
But that, I've learned, is just a pretty lie.
I sit upon my throne, and play my part
With chilling dread still hanging 'round my heart.

THE LAST OF HAMELIN

How many minutes, how many hours passed
Since that day the Piper played his flute,
And led the children of my town away?

The mayor and all his councilmen are gone –
The words engraved above their bones are fierce.
They'll never be forgiven for their greed,
Though maybe, when that mountain turns to dust,
They'll earn the grace to simply be forgot.

I am the last one living from that time,
And there are fewer days ahead of me
Than all the days that stretch so long behind.
I was a child, then. And yes, I heard.
And yes, I felt the tugging at my heart.
I longed to follow, but, because I'm lame,
I was forced to stay behind and watch
My fellow children dancing down the street
And through that magic door to who knows where.

My mother always feared I would get hurt
If I joined in my neighbors' boisterous games.
And so, on sunny days, when laughter rang,
She kept me in, where I'd be safe, upstairs.
But they – my friends – remembered me, that day.
They paused their dance, turned back, knocked at our door
And told me to come down, and not to fret:
If I grew tired, I could piggyback.
They'd carry me, they promised, taking turns.

In spite of her, I hurried down the stairs.
But oh – alas! My 'hurry' was too slow,
The pull of that sweet melody, too strong.
They could not wait. Like leaves upon the stream
My friends were swept away, and I was left
With all the adults by the empty street
The moment when that magic portal closed –
A thunderclap that echoed through the air
And made our houses chime like mighty bells.

I barely had a breath of silence, then,
Before the questions landed from all sides.
They demanded: "What was it you heard?"
"What promises were made within those notes?"
"What shining world could lure them all away?"
And "Did he make a promise just for you?
Did the Piper promise you'd be cured –
That you could run, without a crutch or limp,
And be a happy child, like the rest?"

I tried to tell them: "Friendship, to the last,
And laughter, too, as loud as you could wish,"
Was all I heard. I tried, but was ignored.
'Twas not until I said I wanted cure,
And yes, that I was sad to still be lame,
That all their questions ceased. And then, they sighed.
They patted my poor head and trundled home.
And after that there were no boisterous games,
So Mother let me out on sunny days.
But even in July, I felt a chill.

I hear it still, you know – inside my head.
Each note, and trill, and pause, all in their place
(As full of promise, beautiful and clear,
As on that dread and fateful day back then).
And even though the Piper's gone away
(His brightly colored coat no beacon, now),
I do my best to follow it, each day,
And scan each face of people that I meet,
In hope of seeing those familiar smiles –
The ones that say: "We want you by our side,
So please join in, and do not fret at all."
And even if I search for my whole life,
If my last breaths are taken in a laugh,
It's not too late.

Tiny Tim

"Now, come on, Tim," they said, quick as they could,
As soon as Father set me to the floor,
"Let's go and hear the Christmas pudding sing,"
We all three knew that look on Father's face,
That I would be the subject of their talk.
The pudding was an honorable excuse,
My Christmas gift: a blessed (if brief) escape.

Those little ones – they never knew a time
Before I used a crutch or wore a frame.
And even though they're taller than myself,
I'm still their older brother, and they're proud
To share their secrets and their games with me.
I never sense the pity or the fear
The way I do with Martha, Belle, and Pete.

My brother laughed and said the pudding bag
Sounded the great big choo-choo train.
And Sister wanted me to say those words
Just like the station man calls "All aboard!"
I said my lines; my mind was somewhere else.

I wonder which of these two sins is worse:
To tell a lie (on Christmas, of all days!),
Or speak the truth – and not believe it so.
I really hate it when the people stare,
Though I can see it hurts my father more.
And so, instead, I said that I was glad –

To reassure him that my life has worth,
And his life, too, to father such a son
(Despite the whispers from the other pews).
I worry, though, how well he will get on;
Who will look after him, when I am gone?

THUMBLING

The people tell me I'm a lucky one,
'Cause even though I am a wish-born child
(Those never come out normal, like you want),
At least I'm human-shaped from head to heel.
Not like that monster, Hans, the next town, over,
Who's just a prickly hedgehog, snout to waist,
So he must spend his life behind the stove,
On a moldy bed of straw, with bugs to eat.
A burden to his father – such a shame!
And then, they start to argue: When's the last
That anyone had caught a glimpse of him?
Some hope he's finally dead, and so at peace.
The people tell me I'm a lucky one,
'Cause even though I'll never grow a whit,
At least I'm handsome, and I'm clever, too.
And I can help to drive my father's cart,
Whispering commands in Dobbin's ear.
They say I'm blessed. I grit my teeth and nod,
Not like that poor boy Hans, the next town over.
My parents love me like a wish come true,
And listen to me when I have ideas.
My father built a bed that's just for me.
My mother stitched a coat that's just my size.
My supper dish may be an acorn cap,
But I have had my fill of bread and cheese.
They tell me to be glad I'm not like Hans.
And I am glad. I wish they'd notice why.

King Hans the Quillback

I've heard the rumors – how my story's told.
First things first: it did not end that way
(My skin all milky white, and hair of gold,
My father proud until his dying day).
And second: tell me, how would I have known
The steps I'd need to take to 'break the spell'
If I'd never left my bed of straw and stone?
As if I'd even want to (go to Hell).
That's just the yarn they spin to quell their fears,
And I've remained a monster – sixty years.

I ran away from home, that much is true.
But never with a gift from 'dear old Dad'.
I stole those bagpipes, and the black hen, too –
The only friend I ever really had.

It's true the king was lost, and heard me play,
Though, like I said: I never had a plan.
But when he told me he would gladly *pay*,
And pulled one of those rings from off his hand …
He asked me if I'd like his "pretty hat"
(Can you imagine – velvet on *my* head?
And really, what would I have done with that?).
But he was loved! I needed that, instead.

So yes, I said: "Give me a living thing –
The first to come and greet you at the door."
I never thought: *the daughter of the king* –
Might be his dog, for I'd seen that, before.

And after that, I let myself forget –
Until the day my dear old chicken died.
That was the first I ever felt regret,
Though not the first time I had ever cried.
I really didn't think 'twould do much good,
To try and claim a worn out IOU,
But there was nothing for me, in that wood,
And there was nothing left for me to do.

They kept their promise – *that's* the magic thing,
When they could have lied, or had me killed.
I married her. And now I am the king,
Though I still have my snout, and all my quills.
For we can't shed our pain, like some old shirt,
To throw onto the coals, until it's gone.
I'm less than half a man, without my hurt
Yet, truly, I was changed, that coming dawn.

'Twas neither flames nor salves that transformed me,
But *she* – who saw my full humanity.

EXPERT OPINIONS

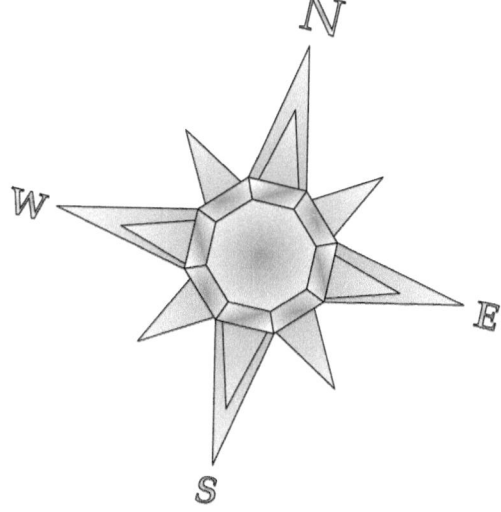

To the Stillborn Janus Calf

One

I've heard that infants, still inside the womb,
Find comfort in the roar of Mother's pulse,
And learn the rhythms of both day and night
From the rocking and the resting in her gait.
I hope, for your sake, this was world enough;
And, without comparison, the stretching womb
Had felt as wide as any summer sky,
By your account: a life as long as Time.
And, if you had felt any sense of self
(Without the mirror of an other's gaze),
That you were comfortable inside your bones,
And never felt the ache that you were wrong.
I hope that self had melted like the fog –
So you'll be spared my voyeuristic verse.

Two

Those who pulled you free to open air
Were no doubt startled by your second face.
That grew, like a reflection, from your skull.
For that distinction, now, your bones shall rest
Within the Field Museum, on a shelf,
Where scientists, for centuries to come,
Shall craft memorials from your remains
To honor all the twists that life can take.
Two women, now, with skill and strength, reveal
Your perfect organs, and your curving bones.

They answer their uneasiness with laughs,
Their voices mixing pathos with disgust:
"My heart leapt just a bit, as when I step
Off of the roller coaster to the ground."

THREE

In ancient Rome, a priest of oracles
Would call you *monstrum* (warning) and proclaim
A grave calamity would soon befall
Unless another life were sacrificed.
To Isidore, Archbishop of Seville,
This warning was a mercy from Our Lord.
But humans, being human, will conflate
The victims of our fear with foul intent.
And anyone whose difference is too strange
Becomes the X a forester would leave
Upon a tree that's destined to be culled:
A stigma on the whole society.
It's best, for all concerned, to seek the cure.
And if we cannot cure, lock them away.

FOUR

I was born alive, with just one face,
But do not move according to the script.
I've heard that mix of pathos and disgust
When strangers in the street dare talk at me.
And so I wonder if, while in the womb,
I could have had a budding sense of self.
Could I have been at ease inside my bones,

Without the inkling I am something wrong,
Before there ever was an other gaze
To view me through that fun-house mirror dread?
Or is it true our selves are only made
From all the scraps this crowded world can give?
Now you, dear one, are part of my collage.
And from your life I'll craft a bit of truth.

GHOST STORY: 1966

This was my mother's own creation myth;
It marked the borders of our universe –
The Hero Tale which sang the primal dance
Between us and Authorities, who could
Reshape our lives as easily as speak.

I was just two, and newly diagnosed,
"Cerebral palsy" written in my chart:
Two words, like lenses in an eyeglass frame,
That altered what the 'experts' saw in me.
The nurse, who grabbed my stroller from behind,
And rushed me down the hall without a word,
Saw just another subject to observe.
The psychologist, who gave the IQ test,
Saw in me another data point;
My baffled silence was his evidence –
Proof enough of everything he knew.
He sent for Mother, in the waiting room,
To give the solemn, devastating, news:
My "mental retardation" was complete,
And I would need an institution's care.
But mother, in her anger at that nurse,
Instead of waiting, had plotted her revenge.

She came in then, and sat down next to me,
Gave me a smile.
The doctor got five words:
Just "Yes," and "No," and "I don't know –" no more.

And this time, with my mother at my side,
I answered all his questions, right on cue.
He crossed out "retardation," with a note
That she had been "manipulating" me –
And was, quite clearly, hostile to him.

As youth rolls on to age, and day to night,
This story haunts me. Like a chaperone,
It brings the ghost they call *What Might Have Been*
To whisper in my ear, until I sleep.

If Mother had been cowed by 'expertise'
(As was expected of a housewife, then),
Would they have wheeled me down the corridor
To walls of cinder-block and rows of beds,
Where the only air is stale, and nothing's kind?
Or if we had been poor?
Or if our skin were dark?
Would Mother's fight have won the battle, then,
Or would defiance render her 'unfit'?
Would I have even lived as long as this?
Or would I be a shade in photographs,
My face blurred out in documentary stills?

The streetlamp shadows fade; I drift awake
Still reaching for the sound of Mother's laugh:
Her punctuation to this story's end.

I, alone, remain to tell it now
And, like some scholar of antiquities,
I'm left with scattered fragments of the past:

27

Worn artifacts once shaped in other times.
I must decipher, best as I know how,
What all these pieces mean, and how they fit,
To tell a story that is too seldom told,
And lay the ghosts that history forgets.

To the Map-Maker

You stand there, with my file in your hand:
A long white coat beneath fluorescent light.
Your voice is measured, your expression, bland
To thinly veil the arrogance of might.
With scientific words, you speak your part;
Your glance betrays a superstitious heart.

As though I were not even in the room
(And near enough to catch stale coffee breath),
You lay out (for my mother) all the doom
Of raising such a daughter so bereft.
For I will never walk as humans can:
Upon two legs, and tall, across the Earth.
With crutch tips as my hooves, I'll cross each span
In trotting gait, because of star-crossed birth.
With practiced stroke and swiftly moving pen
(Just as you've done with other children's lives),
You mark me down as something less than 'man'
To fit me to a list that you've contrived.
You circumscribe my life in dark blue ink.
My flesh and mind are mapped (or so you think).

The Challenge

There came a nightmare day that woke us all
From the idyllic dream we were immune
To all the terror invading lives abroad:
'Twas two thousand nine hundred ninety-six,
The count of human lives to meet their end
On that most jewel-like, sweet, September day.

Then, from that nightmare sprang a brand new dream:
A fleet of saviors – all impervious
To toxic air, and radiation's teeth,
To navigate our newly-shattered world
And find, and flip the switch, and close the valve,
Thus holding back disaster just enough

To save more lives.

The robotics engineer explains his plan:
"There is a reason all stairs are just so high,
And handles on the doors are where they are:
Our world is made to fit our human kind,
And so the robots must be human-shaped
If they are to succeed in all their tasks."

But there exist so many human lives
Whose body shapes the architects forget –
Who neither climb the stairs, nor open doors.
And often, when their private nightmare comes,
They then are told to wait out of the way.
They're promised: "Rescue's coming." In the end

It often comes too late.

Remember: every door and every stair
Is built deliberately, and with intent.
What does it mean to have a 'human' shape?
What does it mean, to build a world that 'fits'?
And when those bodies and those worlds collapse,
Then what shape will we choose for days to come?

From a Documentary on Science

"It is miraculous," the surgeon says,
"To place electrodes deep within the brain,
And see these patients, trembling in their chairs,
Each stand and walk, like normal people do,
And so regain their human dignity."

The television host across from him
Nods placidly, with just the slightest smile.
The lighting, and the set, and cutaways,
All make it seem impossible to doubt
His words or deeds or hopes for all mankind.

But, still –

Perhaps it was like Santa Claus, you know,
A pretty fable Mother told to me,
To soften life's hard edges for my sake,
When she had said that dignity was mine –
For me, alone, to squander or to keep.

But now I've learned the gray and dreary truth:
Whatever makes me worthy of esteem
Is held completely in the public trust
Revocable without recourse or right,
When strangers, in disgust, avert their eyes.

ADVICE FOR LIVING WITH CEREBRAL PALSY

It's natural to feel a certain rage,
Those times your doctors do not understand
That your condition changes as you age,
Dismissing what you say, right out of hand.
We know it seems as if they just don't care –
Don't even want to listen to your voice.
But when you feel that Life does not play fair
Remember that you always have a choice:
Just think a calm, relaxing, happy thought,
For no one wants to help you, when you're mad.
Professionals do all the things they ought,
And worry leads to outcomes that are bad.
Don't risk the pain of beating on that wall.
For you're the one who's broken, after all.

A Word of Caution

Protection from the superstitious thought
Is not achieved through high technology,
Nor knowing obscure names for body parts,
Your long white coat, or medical degree.
And though your teachers, all, used piercing minds,
With scientific rigor, to unfurl
The tangled shroud of ignorance which binds
The future hopes and dreams of this poor world,
The superstitious thought was still passed on
Whenever false assumptions went unchecked.
It may be dormant, but not completely gone:
Infection spreads from one class to the next.
You swore an oath to strive for public good.
But does that mean just what you think it should?

STICKS AND STONES

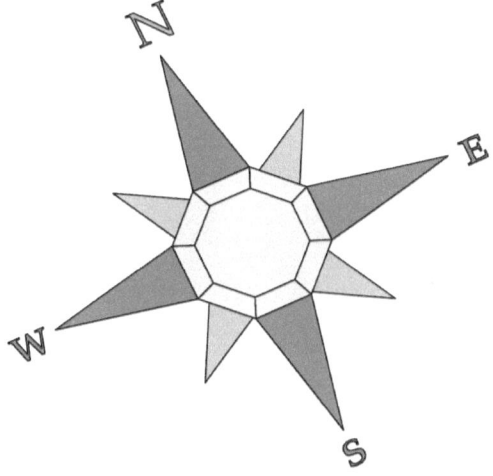

REBUTTAL

Well, sticks and stones can also make a house:
Four sturdy walls to shelter us from storms,
A door to latch against the noisy world,
Or open wide, to welcome in a friend.
And sticks and stones can also form a bridge:
A graceful arch above the churning flood,
Or mark the road, to help us find the way,
Or be the prayer upon a loved one's grave.
It's words, alone, give order to our days;
They map our minds, and set the laws of kings.
Though weightless as a shadow, they endure.
The things we do not name we do not see.
And neither stick nor stone has cracked a bone
Before a scornful word has set the aim.

WAR OF WORDS

It's a tragic story that we love to tell:
How children, in their native cruelty,
Wield words like pitchforks, broken glass, and stones,
How playgrounds turn to battlegrounds
And some
Will never make it out of there alive.

We only have ourselves to blame, of course.
As adults, it's our job to keep control,
And never let the violence break through.

We try again, and trade those misused terms
For words made safe for younger minds to hold.
We pad them thick with extra syllables,
And add a bright veneer of innocence,
Like: 'special', 'touched', and 'just a little slow'.
We sit the young ones down at Circle Time,
Between the alphabet and morning snack.
With voices sweet as medicine, we try
To introduce them to a brand new friend,
Whose name is 'pity', then we humbly ask
This friend to drive the hatred from our schools.

> I am the Angel Pity.
> Please let me be your guide.
> And let's pretend I am not Hate,
> Just wearing Mercy's hide.
> I'll teach you how to have restraint,
> And not use all your powers,

How not to squash the lowly worms
That crawl among the flowers.
They cannot help it, being worms.
And though they are disgusting,
We all must treat them gently, dears,
And keep them sweet and trusting.
For if they roared, as lions do,
The world would fall apart.
And so I ask you to restrain
The hatred in your heart.

But children, in their play, are
Unrestrained.
We hear the new-coined phrases
That we'd so carefully taught
Enunciated, emphasized, and clear.

But somehow, now, they
Have a cutting edge,
Like pitchforks, broken glass, and stones.
The playground armistice never lasts.
Whatever happened to childhood innocence?
Have these kids no pity?

We might as well be Sisyphus,
Rolling that rock uphill,
Or try to reverse the pull of gravity.
They're only kids –
It's just the way they are;

We'll coin new phrases, though, and try again.
As adults, it's our job to keep control.

Except you can't deny that it's absurd
To be so damned PC about some words.

HANDICAPPED

Soon after the Eleventh Hour passed,
Before the trench-scarred earth could feel the plow,
Parades were held to mark our victory,
And monuments erected for the dead.
But beneath each waving, patriotic, flag,
The new-born century's hope had turned to fear.
And for the over hundred thousand men
Who had returned from fighting Over There,
And kept their lives, but lost their limbs or sight,
There were no words of praise nor time for grief.

Our nation's future called for confidence,
With new assembly lines to build, and run –
The wheels of Progress must forever roll.
We could not risk our young Democracy
By dwelling on injustices, or loss.
And wounded bodies, now, were question marks:
How could you be a man, and be in pain,
Or one iota less than strong and free?
And in those places where the blood spilled out
Could foreign and seditious thought seep in?

The orders came from generals to the ranks:
Remember that you're in the Army, still.
Your duty to the country is to fight,
And *normalcy* the ground you must retake.
Recovery must be both swift and sure,
And you must show your cheerful gratitude.
You must not think that you have paid enough.

Now, this is voluntary. You are free
To take the jobs we will retrain you for,
Or lose your benefits, and all your pay.

Photographers would come to capture them,
With smiling Red Cross nurses by their beds,
Their bodies framed as emblems to inspire.
One word appeared with growing frequency
Meant just for them, in captions underneath.
Before they'd left for war, they'd seen it used
For those defective children who can't learn
And by the colored men who spoke of hate:
A word that meant "a burden, and a shame" –
A burden they must strive to never be.

In days gone by, it had a different weight:
A sporting word to even up the odds,
Where fathers bantered, laughed, and put down bets
(The air thick-scented with horses and the turf).
But now, those golden memories felt like lies,
For none of them gave their consent to this.
The exhortations to recall their pride,
And rhetoric that spoke of useful work,
Were not enough to quell their growing rage:
The sense that, now, their race through life was fixed.

CRIPPLE

It's just a word,
That, aimed in my direction, grows fangs:
A living weapon, guaranteed to wound.
I've been lucky, though. Mostly,
It just whizzes past my ears
With every news report
(Nations' economies, *crippled* by debt,
And transportation infrastructure, *crippled* by neglect)
To fall, impersonal as a pebble,
On the ground.
The headline writers who've chosen it,
Again and again, plead innocence.
It's just a tag for lifeless things: –

Useless and unwanted as they are,
And only fit to be repaired.

It's my responsibility, I'm told,
To forget the human targets.
(Who all died long ago, anyway
Might as well be make believe).
If I slip upon the gravel path
This word has made,
If I should fall, and feel the thousand cuts,
It's my own damned fault.

One day, I reached the limit of my tolerance.
I longed to see Cripple's sinew, and its bone
Spread before me, and labeled well,

To prove (to myself, if no one else)
Its fangs are real, and they still bite.
Instead, upon the dictionary page,
Below the definition (noun and verb),
Deep within its Anglo-Saxon roots,
I only saw witness to a human condition:
First, the word for *bent*, as in "contracted limb,"
And then, the word for "crawl upon the ground."

Here was an outline so much like myself
It might have been the hollow in my bed
I leave behind when morning comes.
An echo from near a thousand years
Before an esteemed surgeon wrote those symptoms down,
And so 'discovered' folks like me exist.

That was the lie I did not think to find.
For I'd been taught my 'challenges' were new.
Within our living memory (so they said),
The babies born too soon, with crooked limbs
Who never learned to walk, but only crawled,
Would be, with conscience clear, allowed to die.
'Twas more than penicillin saved my life,
More, even, than the incubator's warmth –
'Twas modern day enlightenment and grace.

How could those lexicographers have known
That they were oracles by accident,
To send me ancient truth from ancient ghosts?

"Please know: we've always lived upon this Earth –
We few, we stubborn few, who made our way;
And even though your history forgets,
Our lives have left their mark upon your tongue."

Cripple was never born for teeth;
Its piercing fangs, like iron spurs,
Were forced upon it
By those who want to see it cowering
And who rejoice to see my people flinch.
Now I only long to set it free
To trade the ragged hand-me-downs it's worn –
Moth-eaten blankets soaked in Pity's tears –
For something better – something warm and soft:
Bright silks of creativity and pride.

A Frank Conversation

Oh, Language, dear, what shall I do with you?
You've charmed, and teased, and soothed my aching heart.
I've loved you all my life – that much is true –
But all the pain you cause tears me apart.
Should I proclaim your virtue to the end,
And argue that they all have done you wrong?
Or should I, like the blacksmith, twist and bend,
And heat, and beat, and quench, to make you strong?
I'd never leave you, even if I could,
You are as much to me as my own breath.
In spite of all your faults, and for your good,
I pray you'll stay with me until my death.
Am I your mistress? Or could you be mine?
The answer's balanced on a shifting line.

IN THE PUBLIC EYE

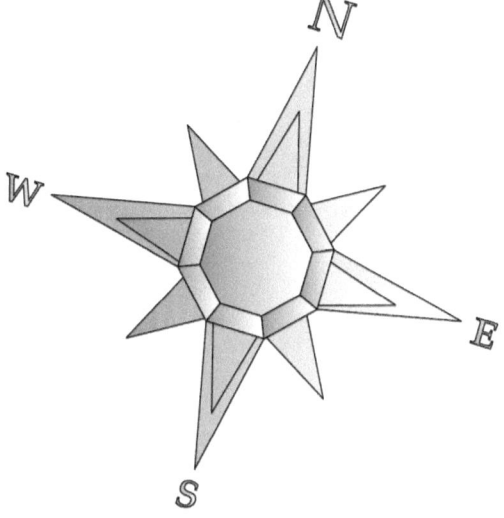

IF AND WHEN

If my grief over Mother's death were a person,
This would be the year it could buy its first drink
With friends at the bar
Slamming the mug down in triumph,
Froth crowning its upper lip.
Then, maybe, there'd be singing.
Or, maybe, my grief, taking after me,
Would be a teetotaler, content
To drift on the rising tide
Of friends' besotted laughter.

If my grief over Mother's death were a person,
I'd make a wish that its friends,
When drunk, would only laugh –
Opening their arms wide for tipsy hugs
And slurred *I love you*s!

I remember the year my grief was born –
Seems like only yesterday, sometimes.
I, a grad student a hundred miles from home,
Rolling across campus in my motorized chair,
Would sing aloud, not caring
If my spastic throat pulled the tune off-key.
I needed to sing, to give my voice
The power to cut through helplessness
Like the prow of an ice-cutter
Through the North Atlantic:

My life flows on, in endless song
Above Earth's lamentation.
I hear the sweet, though far off, hymn
That hails the new creation.
Above the tumult and the strife
I hear its music ringing.
It sounds an echo in my soul.
How can I keep from singing?

Of course I got noticed.
Moving through the cafeteria,
The song's final notes trailing behind me,
I'd overhear: "She's such an inspiration –
Always so happy!"

The irony sparked
Even through my grief-fogged mind.

This woman: my mother,
Daughter of a mathematician,
Graduate of the Bronx High School of Science,
Asked me to work magic on her behalf –
To arm myself with hope and vision,
To battle at her side from a hundred miles away.
Whether she believed the power of thought
Could alter the progress of her cancer,
Or merely deflect the pity and disgust
That oncoming death inspires,
I do not know.

But when I was two, this woman, my mother
Refused to be cowed by the hospital psychologist
And saved me from a life behind institutional walls.
When I was eight, she taught me
How to write a letter of protest.
She hand delivered it to my teacher
At the PTA meeting, that night.
The next morning, I learned that the authority of justice
Could make the authority of position tremble.
When I was thirteen, in the spring of seventy-seven,
We rallied together under hand-painted signs
So that I (and others) could roll across campus.

(While waiting for the elevator,
An acquaintance finds the courage to ask
If I dream of walking, or hope for a cure.
I say there is no cure. And anyway,
I'd rather spend my numbered days
Out in the world, writing stories, or teaching children,
Then behind the walls of a physical therapy gym.
My answer earns rebuke
For "giving in to my disability.")

When I was sixteen, Mother fought our town hall
For a wheelchair access ramp,
And cut the ribbon at the opening ceremony,
The mayor smiling at her side.
"I will support you in anything
You decide to do," she told me, years later –
"But it is up to you to decide it."

And so, for her sake, I sang
And told no one the reason.

> The water's wide, and I can't cross over.
> And neither do I have wings to fly.
> But give me a boat that will carry two
> And both shall row
> My love and I.

Reincarnation, she once said, happened
When daisies pushed up from the grave,
And bugs ate the flowers, and birds ate the bugs.
She assured me that the energy of her life,
(Like the energy of an electron) would be conserved –
And if I needed to, I could find her
In the downbeat stroke of a crow's wing.

In those first years, my grief demanded
All my attention, and care.
Now, there are long stretches of silence between us
But it still wanders home in the middle of the night
Waking me from dreams.

For twenty-one years,
I have watched for the shadows of crows.
And told no one the reason.

Until now.

– OCTOBER 27, 2012

Open Question, Open Door

"Why are you in that thing?" the child asks,
Wide-eyed and pointing
(Were my hands and fingers ever so small?).
"My chair?" I ask. He nods. And I explain:
"I just have a disability," I say.
"My legs don't move the way I want,
So I use this chair instead of walk."
"Is it fun?"
"Sometimes … You know what I like best?"
"What?"
"Puddles. I like to drive through puddles,
And make them splash,
And then to make designs with my tire prints."
He giggles. "Yeah. Me too," he says.

He returns his attention
To his finger-food kid's meal.
With a little more room at the table
For people like me.

CHALLENGE TO YOUR CATEGORIES

The day is warm, the playful breeze is light;
The sun (just like a lover at the gate)
Has called the flowers out – and you, as well –
So even mundane tasks are pleasant things.
And then, you see the shadow in the crowd:
A monster in the corner of your eye.

An insult made of flesh and bone – obscene!
Worse than any word or gesture, this:
Audacity in daring to exist:
Denying everything you know is true.
And you are Good. You've learned what elders taught.
About what makes a Man, and makes a Beast,
And how to tell an Adult from a Child,
And how to keep your own place in the world.
The monster in the crowd has moved away.
The shadow that it cast remains behind;
It's lodged there, in the corner of your thoughts –
A seed that's far too dangerous to sprout.
But you are Good. You take this as a test,
Enclose what's Wrong in pity, and move on.

Small Talk

It's weird, but I suppose it might be kind,
When strangers ask me this, out of the blue –
Acknowledgment I have an inner mind,
(When all they see is what I cannot do).
I know the answer that they wish to hear
(Their desperate longing leaks between the seams).
But I must tell them something else, I fear:
"Not really, no. I never walk in dreams."
I leave it there, instead of going on:
"Except, of course, when nightmares bother me."
For in my mind, 'twixt midnight and the dawn,
My walking means "coerced conformity."
In really happy dreams, I belly-crawl:
True to myself, my body, brain, and all.

SHUTTERED WINDOWS

The elevator lift into my van
Was always slow and clanking loud –
Seemed worse on winter days
In damp north wind.

But it was never so slow
As in that moment
On that
Warm
Summer
Afternoon.

The three of them:
White-haired white men,
Sitting in the bed of the green pickup truck
The next space over, watched
As my aide lowered the lift
And I got on:
Their eyes
Trained on me
As I rode up,
Each gaze like
The muzzle of
A double-barrel
Shotgun

Poking through the curtains
Of a locked-up house.

The Voice of Reason

There are no monsters underneath the bed
(Or so they say). They say there never were.
And when a baby's born with half an arm,
No chanting priest foretells the death of kings.
Today, we know the scientific truth.
And we've outgrown those silly, antique, tales.

(Or so they say). And yet, we're all afraid.
There's *something* churning underneath our feet.
This modern world is bursting at the seams,
And all agree that order must be kept.
We've turned to science, and learned ten thousand ways
To know just who is normal and who is not.
We raise our funds, we look for cures, invent,
And teach the child to wear a plastic arm.
And though we know it's fiction, we still cheer
The knight's triumphant ride, returning home;
At last, the dragon's dead, and now her heart
Is safely bundled in his handkerchief.
The monsters must not ever win the fight.
But they must try (and fail) to prove *we're* right.

THE ENCOUNTER

I navigate the steepness of the path
As gravel slides beneath my rolling wheels,
To join the stranger standing on the bank,
And share, in silence, the beauty of this place.
The curve of Highlands across the river's breadth,
The murmur of the water against stone,
The golden blush of light that fills the sky,
All this helps me forget the ticking clock.

"How long have you been in that chair?" he asks.
I answer without thinking: "All my life."

"How sad," he says.

His words have hit me like a sudden punch.
I mutter: "Actually, it's really not."
But he's already going on his way,
His need to pity me now satisfied.

The words he spoke, however, hold their ground.
To squat, with all their kindred, in my mind.

My anger follows quickly after shock
For he belittled both life's pain and joy.
And I remember friends who've always walked
But suffered families who could not give their love.

And as the passing years have since unfurled,
I have replayed this meeting in my mind,

And thought of clever things I should have said
(A comfort of some sort, like counting sheep).

But now, a second question nags at me:
Why did I even answer him at all?
As if my words were something that I owed,
Each dropped like quarters into a machine,
To purchase just a bit of due respect?

AN EMERGING SENSE OF SELF

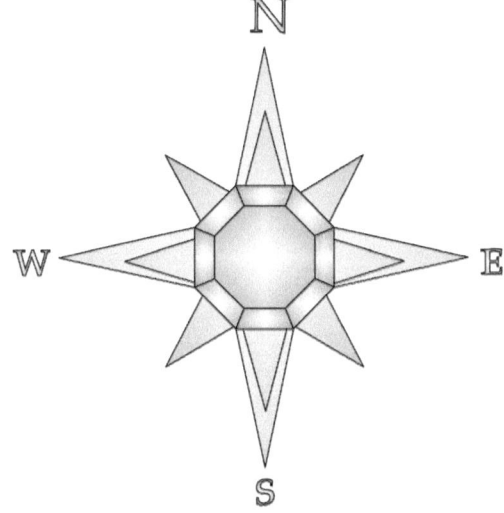

EARLY EDUCATION

I learned to tell a story at age three
(At least, the craft of pacing and suspense).
Propped up between my parents on the couch,
With season one of "Star Trek" on the screen.
Although I could not hide, I quickly learned:
Anticipate the music's minor shift,
Then plug my ears, and close my eyes, and hum
Until the things that scared me went away.
I never feared the aliens as much
As all the angry shouts and lasers' whine.
It always happened – every episode –
As soon as any "monster" came on screen.
Could I have understood this (still so young):
My difference, too, is something that they fear?

A Good Fit

For some, the world fits like a tailored suit.
They trust that they can slip into a room
And that the space will drape so easily
Their shoulders hardly feel the weight at all.
And every sentence seamlessly unfurls
Its meaning to their minds without a snag.
As best they can recall, there's been no need
To notice where the edges don't quite match,
Or where there is a tangle, or a pinch.

Except for us, the patterns do not fit.
So, carefully, we thread our way between,
Each cutting knots, and fixing jagged seams
With homemade shears and needles that we find.
Thus, stitch by stitch, we fashion our own lives.
We shift the space. They notice *that*, and frown,
And tug their collars with itchy discontent.
But when they come upon the trails that we have blazed,
They'll find a world made graceful through our craft.

Out of the Labyrinth

In looking down upon my naked self:
My lap, my scars, my hands, and crooked feet,
My posture's slant, my elbow's inner bend,
I sometimes wonder what it means to see.
This "looking at myself from where I am"
Is not at all like looking at a stone.

The words that rustle in my memory –
Like forest leaves that shift in every wind –
Their shadows hide – disguise – what I have learned.
So I must wander through this tangled wood
To find my truth, and know just what I am.
And then: one word. It catches like a thorn.
I trace its growth. And there, I find the root:
That *monster*, once, meant "Warning from the gods:
A birth gone wrong." Well, that's been said of me.
And now, it's clear: the dread in strangers' eyes
Is just a nightmare's echo, nothing more.
One shadow pierced; this light shall answer fear.
And here's the fruit: it's heavy – rich with seed.
I'll plant one for myself, and start again.

There Comes a Time

There comes a time when nothing is enough.
My mind, poor starven wretch, sits at the feast,
And hunching, double-fisted, tries to stuff
Her loneliness with everything in reach:
Old jokes, odd dreams, or memories of Fall,
My coffee cup, the weight of falling rain –
Like Tantalus inverted, gobbling all –
Her torment is that hunger will remain.
From sheer exhaustion, then, my mind grows still,
And in one breath, she quenches every thirst.
The pause between each word begins to fill
With all Earth's shining beauty: last to first.
This poet's muse has called my poor mind's bluff.
And shown the truth: that "nothing" is enough.